Living
Holistic Wellbeing

by
Sue Tew

All proceeds from the sale of this book are donated to animal welfare

Living food for holistic wellbeing © Copyright Sue Tew 2011.

This book does not presume to offer medical advice or advice of any other nature. All information contained in this book is for information purposes only. It is not intended in any way as a substitute for professional medical advice, diagnosis or treatment. It comes from the personal experience of the author.

Your health and wellbeing is your personal and legal responsibility at all times and any decisions you choose to make about it are solely yours. In respect of your health and wellbeing the qualified opinion of a medical/health professional should always be sought.

DEDICATION

This little book is dedicated to Vanya Maw, the woman who changed my life. Vanya taught me more than she will ever know. She showed me the way forward into a world filled with vibrant health and wellbeing where I can be the best I can be. Vanya asked nothing of me other than I share the knowledge she gifted me with others. I hope this book as it reaches those who need it, will do this.

Vanya - my gratitude is boundless. I hold you in the light and bless you always.

INTRODUCTION

Every aspect of 'you' starts with the food you eat. It's the fuel for life and I believe there is no truer saying than 'you are what you eat'. This little book offers you the opportunity to experience your wellbeing in a natural, balanced way through living food.

The food you put into your body and how it affects you has more far reaching consequences than you may think. You are an holistic being, made up of the elements of mind, body, spirit and emotions. What you eat can affect every element of your life. Eating a predominantly raw food diet will fill you with vibrant energy and bring you the opportunity to be the best you can be. You are a unique being, responsible for caring for yourself and your needs at all times. Natural balance and vitality is your birthright. You carry an immense, holistic resource bank within you. Are you using it?

The information in this little book offers you the opportunity to start thinking about how well you are right now and what changes you might want to make to rebalance your life and be the best you can be.

It comes to you with love and blessings.

CONTENTS

Chapter 1 Basics to begin with

Chapter 2 Storage and preparation

Chapter 3 Equipment

Chapter 4 Taking control - conscious eating

Chapter 5 Introducing living foods to your body

Chapter 6 A clean colon and rehydration

Chapter 7 When, where and how to eat

Chapter 8 Living food and sustainable weight

Chapter 9 Making your own choices

Chapter 10 Having the confidence to change

Appendix 1

Food list - what counts as living food?

Appendix 2

About the author

CHAPTER ONE

BASICS TO BEGIN WITH
Defining raw/living food

Terminology

I use the terms 'raw food' and 'living food' interchangeably. I first heard about 'living' food when I became unwell whilst back packing in New Zealand. I did my own thing with it (to greater or lesser degrees) for six years and nourished my body with it so that I became well without surgery.

I didn't realise there was a whole community of people out there engaging with living food. When I did connect with that community I found people calling what I had always known as 'living' food 'raw' food. For my purposes here the terms are interchangeable. They mean the same.

What is living food?

'Basic' living food is fresh, uncooked, preferably organic, fruit, vegetables, nuts and seeds. All are prepared to ensure they retain their natural enzyme and oxygen content (see complete listings of what is mainly included in a living food diet in Appendix 1).

Prepared in ways that allow the body to metabolise food for its maximum benefit, living food promotes optimum energy, vibrant health and wellbeing. This gives the body the nutrients it needs to thrive. An appropriate use of the right combination of living foods will also promote weight loss and sustain weight balance on a permanent basis. Yes, living food is great for reducing weight - but it brings you so much more. It has the potential to open doors you never dreamed of in terms of holistic wellbeing.

What does 'diet' mean?

For the purposes of this book the term 'diet' refers only to food intake. It is only related to weight reduction where this is stated.

Where does the idea of eating raw come from?

The idea of eating raw food is far from new! That's what makes it so easy to connect with. Raw food is the most natural food we can give our bodies. We've been eating it since the beginning of time. Because the enzymes and oxygen have not been destroyed by cooking, our bodies know exactly how to process it in the most effective way.

Nevertheless, for economic reasons, food production and sales have become increasingly complex, especially since the 1950's. This means that, although eating raw is as old as time, we have moved further and further away from the idea as we have moved increasingly towards eating processed, dead, nutritionally deficient foods.

Types of living food

The food list in Appendix 1 shows the main food types you will be increasing in your diet when you start eating living food. The foods listed in each category are by no means exhaustive. However, they give you an idea of some of the key foods you are likely to introduce (or increase in your diet) on a daily or weekly basis when you 'go more raw'.

The quality of your raw food

It's always best to aim to eat good quality live produce. It's all the better if you can grow your own! Choose organic when you can. Organic produce is legally regulated in the UK and requires certification from the Soil Association. The Soil Association mark means the producer must be able to show a traceable history through the production of that food. Choose local produce where possible. Locally produced food will not have been subject to shipping/air freight carriage. It will, therefore, be much fresher and more nourishing. Once it gets out of the ground, the sooner food gets into your body the better it is for you! Nutrients and oxygen in food deplete over time that's what you're witnessing when it starts to wilt and decompose.

Don't eat 'tired' food. It will give you less energy. Ripening food in your fruit bowl is not the best thing to do. It won't gain any nutrients from your fruit bowl! Buy ripe! Eat ripe! And be aware that eating unripe food makes your body work unnecessarily hard to metabolise your nourishment.

Eat fruits and vegetables in season for optimum nutrition. This links to using local produce. In the winter there is still plenty of choice for you to chop up or juice so that you can ensure you continue with your raw intake. Whatever the season, any form of cooking, including pasteurization, usually destroys 100% of the enzymes and most of the vitamins in fresh fruit and vegetables.

Where and how to buy living food

The really good news is that there is now a wider choice than ever of where to buy your living food. You can buy a wide variety of organic living foods in supermarkets today. You may find your local greengrocer stocks some local organic produce too. Look for the freshest produce at the point of purchase and go for organic fruit and vegetables grown locally as a first choice. Buy little and often rather than stocking up. This means your food will always be the freshest possible.

As raw food awareness has grown in recent years a significant number of alternative ways to buy living foods has emerged. As well as supermarkets, organic food stalls, farm shops and farmers markets, there are now web based sites offering local organic box deliveries to your home or workplace. Investigate.

You might like to ask around locally to see if anyone has an allotment and would be willing to sell you some of their produce on a regular basis. In my experience it's common for allotment producers to find they have too much for their own needs.

All good health food shops should stock a variety of seeds and grains for sprouting and a good range of organic nuts and dried fruits. Check out your supermarkets for these as well. You could also try growing some of your own fresh produce if you feel inclined and have the facilities.

Growing your own can be achieved even in the smallest accommodations without a garden. Why not try using growing trays. These can be especially helpful if you want to juice your own freshly cut wheatgrass (the sprouted grass of the common wheat plant). Wheatgrass is packed with chlorophyll, amino acids, enzymes, vitamins and minerals. You can't eat it raw, but when you harvest it fresh in your own kitchen and juice it immediately this super food gives you such an amazing range of concentrated nutrients it will probably make you feel growing your own is well worthwhile - however small a space you have.

Sprouted seeds are a highly nutritious, living, vibrant foodstuff. Buy them in your local health food shop or grow your own. Or, you can even buy these in most good supermarkets now too. It's really easy to sprout your own though (also see Chapter Three - 'sprouting equipment').

More health food shops and supermarkets are starting to stock a wider variety of grains, nuts, fruits and seeds than ever before. There are also a number of websites offering this service if you can't find what you want locally. A quick browse on the net will bring them up in abundance if that's how you prefer to shop.

Having fun matters!

'Your food should be fun'! This really matters. Buying it should be fun! Preparing it should be fun! Eating it should be fun! If you have fun with your food and experience joy with it, you will benefit from it so much more. Experiment with raw, prepare it with love, share it with friends, eat it with pleasure, and always give gratitude for the wonderful gifts the planet gives up - the gifts of nourishment and life.

Love your food and energise your life.

CHAPTER TWO
STORAGE AND PREPARATION
Storing fresh food

When you start eating living foods you are likely to find you want to buy a bigger refrigerator (but think of the lower utility bills as you aren't using the oven to cook!). Keeping fresh foods cool prolongs shelf life (but remember to buy little and often rather than stocking up and trying to prolong shelf life). Latch onto the thought I gave you earlier....As soon as living food is pulled from the ground or plucked from the tree/vine/bush it begins to deteriorate.

Storing dried foods and oils

Buying little and often applies to nuts and oils too. Many people don't realise the relative speed with which these high fat foods deteriorate. This is because they appear (to the eye) to have a long shelf life. Don't be fooled. Don't buy in large quantities unless you will be using them in large amounts quite quickly.

Foods with a high fat content will deteriorate relatively quickly. Always try to buy oils in a dark bottle as this will preserve the quality more than a clear glass container. Store them in a cool, dark, place.

For storage of dried goods airtight glass containers are preferable. Keep them in cupboards out of the light. Plastic isn't ideal. Minor toxins may infiltrate foods stored in plastic containers for long periods of time.

Preparing living foods

Apart from washing under cold running water or in a solution of Himalayan sea salt (or other quality salt) and water if you prefer, or if you feel there may be deposits you need to shift for certain e.g. chemicals or soil residues, you should do as little as possible to your fresh living foods. Less is definitely more in this case. The less you do to living food the more enzymes remain intact and go into your body. When it comes to different methods of preparing raw food for eating there are lots of options to choose from.

Here are just a few of the ways you might prepare living foods:

- *Chop*
- *Grind*
- *Blend*
- *Slice*
- *Dice*
- *Mix*

- *Grate*
- *Mince*
- *Process (in a food processor)*
- *Juice*

For more intricate raw food recipes you may find you use more than one method of preparation.

However you choose to prepare your living foods you should eat them as soon as possible after preparation. As soon as you cut into raw food the enzymes begin to break down. Fresh and as unadulterated as possible is the best way to eat raw food if you want to ensure your body gets maximum benefit from it.

The energy you invest in your food

I would like to add an important note here about the spirit in which you prepare your living food. Although this is part of conscious eating (see Chapter 4) it can also benefit you to think about it at the point of purchase and preparation. If you buy and prepare your food with love and a warm and generous spirit of gratitude this will be the energy you invest in it. It is this energy you will be putting into your body. Sceptical? Why not try it?

Dehydrating fresh food

Dehydrating living foods is now quite common. You'll find a wide variety of dehydrators on the market (check the internet for best buys). Dehydrated food is heated at temperatures below the 118°F at which enzymes are destroyed. Many commentators now class vegetable and fruit based raw food which has been dehydrated as living food.

Dehydrating can bring more variety to a raw food eating plan but it also reduces the water content of the food and condenses the nutritional content (sugar in the case of dried fruits).

Water plays a large part in optimising well being. For me, this means that reducing water content flies in the face of the rehydration of the body unless dehydration is used sparingly. Further to this, if you aim to lose weight, remember that water can assist weight loss.

It's up to you whether you choose to eat dehydrated food and the quantity you feel is appropriate. Whatever your goal, if you do choose to eat a proportion of dehydrated food I'm confident that you will find keeping to small amounts and eating more fresh, living food is beneficial.

If you do choose to dehydrate your food, my suggestion is that you limit your intake of food prepared in this way.

CHAPTER THREE
EQUIPMENT
WHAT DO YOU NEED TO GET STARTED?

A good sharp knife!

A good sharp knife is your starter kit! Everything else is 'extras'. You can add to your equipment as you go, at whatever pace you wish. But to begin your raw food journey all you need is the will to change to a vibrant lifestyle and a good sharp knife (and the most important of these is the will to change to a vibrant lifestyle).

Here are some ideas on equipment you may want to add to your kitchen as you ditch your microwave, oven and hob.

None of the following are essential items so don't feel you have to rush out and invest in anything except that sharp knife. These are items of equipment you may want to consider along the way.

Sprouting equipment

When you're ready I suggest your next piece of equipment should be a sprouting jar. This is because sprouted seeds and beans give you immediate, live, vibrant food that adds a great nutty taste to all water based raw food combinations and doesn't need to cost a penny if you have a couple of old glass jars hanging around.

It's very easy to sprout seeds at home. All you need is a jar, some gauze/net (for a lid) and an elastic band to hold the gauze securely in place. The big glass sweet jars from the old style candy shops are great for larger amounts of sprouting. I'm not going into detail here but soaking seeds overnight, draining and washing them is a very simple process and brings you wonderfully fresh and very live food. To find out more do an internet search for 'sprouting seeds'. There's lots of information out there.

Juicers

A juicer is a great addition to your raw food kitchen as you can condense the amount of living enzymes you get into your body by juicing your vegetables.

Juicers aren't cheap, but don't skimp when you buy one. There are lots of different juicers on the market but most of those you buy in the shops are not up to effectively extracting the maximum amount of juice from vegetables. Save up and invest in a really good model that will do all you want it to do.

If you are planning to juice wheatgrass take care before purchase. Lots of juicers don't juice wheatgrass effectively. You will need to do your homework and research this. See the internet for choices and more information before purchase.

Blenders

Blenders can be bought fairly cheaply in your local electrical appliances store. Like everything else, there's a range of models and you can pay a lot if you want to. Mine isn't a top model but it serves the purpose well enough and I've never felt the need to invest in a super expensive blender!

Food mixers

This is one to research and consider carefully before you go shopping for it. I've had my food mixer for a very long time and it has stood the test of heavy use over the years. However, I use it minimally now as I try to do as little as possible to my living food before eating it. But if you want to chase down the plethora of recipes on the internet you may feel the need for a mixer fairly early on. Do a search for 'raw/living food recipes' and you will be amazed at how much there is out there. It's best to have a good look around, and ask friends who have mixers. Maybe you already have one you've been using for years for cooked food preparation?

Dehydrators

A dehydrator is something you may or may not choose to use. Check out the range of models available.

As with a juicer, it's best to save up and get the one you want or you will probably end up having to buy a better one at a later date as you become more ambitious with your recipes and your food preparation skills develop. This is not likely to be a piece of equipment you rush out to buy when you go more raw (I hope). It's probably best to move into the basic living food way of life before you get a more sophisticated interest and move into the intricate recipe stage.

CHAPTER FOUR
TAKING CONTROL - CONSCIOUS EATING

So - what is conscious eating?

Conscious eating is about being aware of what you are eating and what it's doing to your body, mind and spirit. Unconscious eating is the opposite of this - it's when you eat, not necessarily when you are hungry, but when the reasons for eating are not about nourishment. Unconscious eating is also the type of eating that will often bring about weight gain, discomfort and a sense of disconnectedness between body, mind, spirit and emotions.

In a wider way, unconscious eating can bring about the sense of a lack of connection with the living planet and the world we inhabit. It can contribute to a lack, or loss, of the sense of 'self' as part of the interconnectedness relating to the earth, its elements, and where we sit in the wider sphere of things.

Whenever you put food into your body you are feeding all elements of your 'self' and your identity. It is important to respect your holistic self and only eat when you are feeding a call for nourishment from your body. You can make the choice to do this whenever you are ready - although it may take a little practice to begin with.

Food is a hugely significant part of your life.

Changing what you eat can be done in conjunction with increasing the respect and love you have for yourself, others and the living planet. This means changing eating patterns. The following tips are a sound basis on which to begin the 'retraining' of your 'self' into conscious eating:

- *only eat when you are hungry - if in doubt take a drink of water and wait 20 minutes to be sure an apparent 'hunger' pang isn't just your body calling for water*
- *if you feel inclined to eat for emotional reasons, step back, take a moment or two and make a conscious decision to nurture your body emotionally instead (a relaxing bath, yoga or something you love doing which is not food related)*
- *eat only when you are prepared to sit down, enjoy the sustenance your food brings, take time, and value it with gratitude*
- *banish all 'dieting' notions based on weight reduction - forget about notions of denial and focus on abundance and your holistic health and well being*
- *acknowledge that you know best how to nourish your body, value yourself enough to take control, and nourish yourself with food you know makes you feel vibrant*
- *choose to award yourself enough self respect to take the time to enjoy being present with your food as you prepare it and feel nourished when you eat it*
- *when you are with your food keep your mind*

focused on your food and the blessing that vibrant, living food is in your life you are blessed to have abundance try not to eat

◆ when you are experiencing 'extreme' emotions e.g. loss, upset, distress, stress or other negative emotions

◆ be kind to yourself in other ways than eating (brisk walking or other physical exercise releases endorphins and helps the return to balance) enjoy every mouthful. You are fortunate that the planet provides the bounty you need to sustain you.

Should you not value it?

stop eating when you have had sufficient to nourish you - save what remains for later

always chew your food well (this prepares your food in readiness for effective digestion)

When weight reduction is a concern

Although it may be good to have a goal in terms of the weight you want to lose, try not to measure progress too often. Instead, focus on how you feel inside rather than what the scales say. If you have experienced a negative notion of yourself as overweight for a long time this may be difficult at first. It will happen, if you make the effort. Try to learn to trust that the changes you are feeling inside will allow your weight to melt away naturally on the outside.

When you focus on your inner self and your holistic wellbeing, your perception of your body image will shift. So, try to focus on how you feel inside rather than on your sense of how your physical body looks. If you choose to focus on the amazing changes that will occur within you as you move increasingly into a living food lifestyle, many more significant changes will manifest quite naturally.

The balance of mind, body, spirit and emotions can begin with the food you eat. Only when you have released yourself from any obsession with your physical body (this happens naturally with the living food approach), and gained the amazing energy raw food brings to your world, will you find clarity and be able to identify your way forward to being the best you can be.

If your weight is an issue for you, taking this approach will allow you to free yourself of any concerns about your weight so naturally that you gradually stop thinking about it. And one day you will realise it isn't an issue in your life any longer and you have set yourself free into a fabulous future free from weight loss worry and filled with vibrant energy!

The 'battles' you have experienced with foods you felt guilty about eating will disappear as you no longer desire these foods because you realise they do not nourish your wellbeing. Emotional balance where food is concerned returns.

Only you can evaluate whether a food is good for you. No food can be judged as good or bad in a general sense....it's all about the choices you make for your health and well being. To realise this you must listen to your body, mind, spirit and emotions, connect with them in conjunction with the food you eat, and decide if a particular food is good for your particular holistic wellbeing or not.

With practice this is perfectly possible. All you have to do is tune in. Respect yourself enough to be fully present when you buy, prepare and eat your food. Your body is where your spirit lives. Caring for it is your responsibility.

You should only eat the food you want to eat in the amounts you choose to eat. It is your basic human right to do this.

I hope you will never allow others to leave you feeling insecure in your choices. You can take control of your own choices right now. It takes a single moment to make that decision about your food and your life. How you choose to nourish your holistic being is your business and nobody else's. The choices are yours.

How do you think about food?

Let's take a little time to think about some of the (less than helpful) myths that have come into being about food. I hope this will raise your awareness of some important factors to consider, and help you move forward with the confidence to make informed choices about what you eat in the knowledge that you are the only person in charge of your eating.

You, and only you, have the right to make the

choices about what you put into your body.

If your weight is an issue for you, then you will find moving to a raw food lifestyle puts you in natural control of your weight as well as your wellbeing. With that in mind let's think about perceptions of food.

What's 'good' food and what's 'bad' food?

In my opinion there is no such thing as good or bad food. Diet regimes will often refer to food as good or bad. This can move into your psyche very quickly so that your perception of food soon begins to be coloured by this black and white way of thinking about it. You start to see some foods as forbidden (and long for them more because it's human to do so).

Why not shift your perception and try looking at food from a nourishment point of view? All food nourishes the body to a greater or lesser extent. Each of us has the power to take responsibility for how we choose to nourish our bodies, and the nourishment we choose has a significant effect on the other aspects of our being. If you doubt this you only have to try eating solely processed foods for a few days. How do you feel? Then eat solely fresh, water based living foods for a few days. How do you feel? Point proven!

Each of us knows how we feel when we eat certain foods. If we choose to eat food that is less nourishing, not only our bodies, but our holistic being is less nourished. Choosing to nourish the body poorly over a longer period of time can result in dis-ease. Sometimes early disease can lead to serious ill health further down the line, whether this is mental, emotional, spiritual, physical, or a combination of these.

When we eat the water based living foods that nourish us properly we thrive and all aspects of our lives improve. We gain the all important self respect which is a key to our confidence in ourselves and we are more energetic. Even if we have been malnourished for a long period (perhaps all of our lives) our wellbeing improves very quickly given a nourishing diet.

The myth of the need for endless variety

Let's think about the myth of needing a wide variety of foods to nourish ourselves. Of course we need a variety of foods to ensure optimal health. But our bodies were not originally designed to cope with the wide variety of processed and cooked foods commonly eaten in significant quantities in the western diet today. And it's only with the introduction of processed and cooked foods that we began to expect such extensive variety.

For years now there has been a wonderfully successful marketing mechanism (backed up by huge advertising campaigns) encouraging us to 'eat this' or 'try that', basing all our choices on what we like the look/taste of, rather than what nourishes us. All has been done with a view to maximising profits as a priority and often at the expense of focusing on ensuring positive approaches to health and wellbeing.

You may find you are so used to cooked and processed foods that you no longer know how to appreciate your food as nourishment. Perhaps your focus is on taste alone? Please think about this. Has this happened to you?

In terms of how much choice you have when you visit the supermarket, think about the packaging and how you make your purchases. Do you base your choices on price when you shop? Do you think about how the food has been produced? Where has it come from?

How many processes has it been subjected to before it reaches the packaging stage? How long has it been in the package? How much suffering have living creatures endured during the food production chain process? What is in the food to enable it to remain on the shelf for so long without deteriorating? I urge you to think about all these things.

Perhaps you feel living food offers you less choice? I urge you to think again. With the vast array of choices available in fresh foods today, and the many living food recipes now at our fingertips (in books and on the internet) there is the great opportunity to choose to eat an extremely varied diet of living food and move into a state of improved health and wellbeing.

How much variety you choose to eat is entirely your decision. Only you can take responsibility, and make the choices that can change your life.

CHAPTER FIVE
INTRODUCING LIVING FOODS TO YOUR BODY

Choosing the right approach

If you are used to a diet largely consisting of toxin laden cooked and processed foods it is advisable to make the change to living foods in a graduated way (unless there are urgent health reasons for not doing so). This will allow your body time to adapt as it lets go of the toxins associated with a cooked and processed diet.

If you decide to take the sudden approach and let go of almost all your cooked and processed foods, replacing them with living foods, your body could experience a sense of shock at the sudden withdrawal of toxins. This may manifest in a variety of ways. Headaches, nausea, dizzy spells, skin eruptions, upset stomach, loose bowel movements or other unanticipated symptoms may be experienced.

Sudden and radical changes to your diet may also affect your mood considerably. Although these symptoms may be seen as positive (as they are related to the cleansing process), they are likely to put you off continuing with the change to living foods. Suddenly denying the body the toxins it's had to manage for years is not necessarily the best way. You may need time to adjust.

If you do choose to take the sudden approach to changing your diet, be prepared for side effects. It may be beneficial to drink at least two to three litres of water a day. This will assist with rehydration and toxin elimination.

Food combining

Living food combinations offer the best possible way for your body to metabolise food. Food combining is largely about ensuring the most effective processing and elimination of food by your body. As living foods are cleaner, enzyme and oxygen enriched foods, it really is a question of what your body is comfortable with in terms of food combinations.

If you are eating a 50%+ raw food diet you can consider the combinations and experiment as you go along. What suits one person may not suit another. Find out what suits you best. Take conscious control of your food and your wellbeing. You are unique. You need to get to know your body and the needs it has.

It's good to be open to ideas from other people. However, when you learn to listen to your own body you will know exactly what it needs and when. This takes a little practice and some experimentation with new ideas, but it's well worth the effort. Check in with your body on a conscious level whenever you eat. Listen and learn.

Food combining and knowing what works for you requires you to experiment. The adage that all fruit should be eaten on an empty stomach no doubt holds good for most people. This is because the sugars in fruit will ferment if eaten after other, heavier foods. So this kind of learning is fairly basic for us all. Other 'learning' will come along the way if you tune in and you are prepared to listen for it.

Once you're eating more raw food you'll find your stomach flattens and does not feel bloated. Your elimination process becomes more efficient. If you eat a food, or a food combination, that doesn't suit you it won't be long before your body gives you a sign (e.g. bloating, gas, constipation). Your body will tell you what it wants and the foods that work best together for you. Your job is to listen consciously at all levels, not just the physical, to the messages it sends you.

CHAPTER SIX
A CLEAN COLON AND REHYDRATION

A healthy colon is vital for wellbeing

In my experience, keeping the colon clean means letting go of old emotions as well as food detritus that may have been hanging around your body for a very long time. The colon is where the negative energies of past experiences are stored.

Colon cleansing (also known as colonic irrigation) can assist on many levels. I invite you to take a few minutes to think about the wider implications of this. If you are moving to a living food diet colon cleansing may improve your sense of wellbeing even more.

A combination of colon cleansing and the move to a living food diet can be extremely powerful. You may find it brings you an even more significant sense of wellbeing if you choose to do both. It's like having a spring clean inside. You are preparing to move into a new area of personal growth and development on all levels of your being.

Cleansing the colon will get rid of all the detritus that's been backing up in your system over years. For best results find a well qualified practitioner to work with and cleanse the colon before you introduce/increase living food intake.

Keeping the colon clean also assists evacuation and supports your entire system to work smoothly.

Love your body.

Keeping your colon clean and nurturing it with living food can bring holistic results that will delight you. You are likely to find your mind, body, emotions and spirit will experience positive knock on effects as your energy lifts.

Fluid intake - vital for optimum wellbeing

One of the best ways to maintain colon health, apart from eating living foods, is to ensure you drink plenty of water. This flushes the colon. The first thing to say about fluid intake is that your body is made up of approximately two thirds water. It needs 2~3 litres of water a day just to maintain all systems at optimum levels under normal circumstances. That means just plain, unadulterated water (or herbal/fruit tea) is essential for wellbeing.

In everyday life we all routinely lose approximately three litres of water a day from our bodies (breathing, urine, defecation, perspiration). That being the case, it's clear that we need to rejuvenate with this significant water requirement for optimum hydration.

When appropriately rehydrated, the body will

metabolise food more efficiently. We each have an amazing system of input, processing and output. The body is super efficient at taking the water and nutrients it needs from the food we eat and extracting water from them. As the body makes water by metabolising food one of the best ways to maintain good hydration is to eat a high proportion of unadulterated water based foods.

Fresh fruit and vegetables are the finest foods we can eat to assist the body with daily rehydration. I leave it to you to consider how seriously your body struggles if your food intake is largely cooked (especially in the microwave) and processed!

It's great if we eat plenty of water based food to hydrate ourselves. Nevertheless, drinking water is also important (get the balance right - too little is not good, too much is not good either - so don't overdo it). Two to three litres a day is recommended by most health and wellbeing experts. Find out what suits your needs! And remember that when you are keeping yourself rehydrated you're also losing body salts so you may want to add a little (no more than half a teaspoon daily) pure, high quality salt to your food intake if you think that appropriate. (See 'The Essential Guide to Water and Salt' by F Batmanghelidj M.D. and Phillip Day, 2008', for more information on the water/salt balance).

Another good reason for drinking sufficient water is that this assists with the evacuation of waste matter (and toxins) from the body. If the body is unable to evacuate waste matter effectively food is stored as fat. Over time the storage of excess body fat and toxins is compounded. This means that, at some point, toxic build up will create disease.

Other fluids

Drink as much herbal or fruit tea as you wish (and count this as part of your 2~3 litres of water a day). Avoid all carbonated drinks, all squashes (mostly sugar laden), tea and coffee. These are stimulants and will interfere with your natural digestive processes.

Don't fall into the trap of thinking that freshly squeezed fruit juices are really good for you because of the fruit connection. You're actually drinking high natural sugar concentrations when you juice fruit. In excess, this isn't great for your body. If you feel the need for fresh fruit juices you can always dilute them with water or, better still, drink vegetable juices and sweeten them with apple, carrot or beetroot. As far as your vegetable juicing goes - just go for it. The greener the juice, the more chlorophyll enriched it will be.

CHAPTER SEVEN
WHEN, WHERE AND HOW TO EAT

Some basic guidelines for wellbeing

There are some basic guidelines that will enable you to get the best out of living foods for both weight loss and wellbeing.

Following sleep (at least 6-7 hours of undisturbed rest is good) your body remains in the detoxification, cleansing and elimination part of its natural cycle until the middle of the day. To assist the process you may choose to only eat water based foods during this time.

Starting your day with fresh fruit or a vegetable juice is ideal. Top up with a small handful of seeds if you feel the need for protein. Liquidised/blended fresh fruit will also give you a good start and a great energy boost (but do leave dairy additives out and keep to water and fruit with ice crushed in it for extra body if you feel the need).

If you are a 'grazer' remember that every time you feed your body it has to work to metabolise the food you eat - so do give it breaks between feeding times! Lunch is a good time to stock up with plenty of salad greens and/or fresh organic vegetables as the main part of the meal (at least three quarters of the food on your plate).

If you add grains and/or beans keep to the one

quarter maximum rule. Making this your main meal of the day is ideal and all those vibrant living enzymes will give you plenty of energy to enjoy your afternoon. Experiment by ringing the changes with all the salad and other vegetables out there and try new recipes - there a hundreds to be found on the internet.

If you are new to raw food and you choose to eat your evening meal as you normally would, try to eat before 8pm. If you can get used to the idea that food does not pass your lips after 8pm you'll find you not only assist your body with its natural cycle and weight loss, but the quality of your sleep is likely to improve as well.

A well rested body combined with a high percentage (in excess of 65%) living food diet is a really good basis on which to build all the other things that will set you on the path to optimum wellbeing and natural holistic balance.

Where and how you eat matters

This may seem a strange heading - but bear with me! Perhaps you have never given this as much thought as you should have in the past?

You may find the following information more advantageous than you think!

Eating your food in a pleasing and peaceful environment allows your body to best assimilate it. Eating 'on the hoof' is never a good idea under any circumstances. We don't live in an ideal world, so if there are times when you feel pressured to eat 'on the go' try to stop and think about how you are valuing yourself if you do this.

Your food is your nourishment and the basis of all that is you. Not giving yourself time to be with your food when you eat can devalue your sense of 'self', whether you realise it or not. Building time into your day for preparing and eating your food allows you time with your body and time to value your food and yourself. You may be amazed at how such an apparently small change in lifestyle can add to your wellbeing - and your enjoyment of your food. You will find this creates a greater sense of overall satisfaction and self nourishment. Just as you nourish yourself with a massage, a facial or any other treat, every time you eat should be a time of acknowledged nourishment.

So, try to take time out and eat your food slowly. Chew it well to assist the digestion and enjoy every mouthful. This way you will find you feel more satisfied on many levels.

Reducing and eliminating meat, dairy and other products

Letting go of meat and dairy products from my world was one of the most liberating and energising things I ever did. My energy improved almost immediately, my skin cleared, allergies I had lived with for years quickly disappeared and my weight dropped off naturally into the bargain. How's all that for a result?

The choice to eat meat and dairy is always yours. If you choose to include some meat and dairy produce as you make the transition to a living food lifestyle it will be beneficial if you limit them. You are trying to promote optimum wellbeing (and possibly healthy weight loss). Significant amounts of meat and dairy produce will undoubtedly hamper both. So eat small amounts (if you must eat it at all) and make sure they are as organic as possible.

Many commentators now acknowledge that the human body is not designed to eat significant amounts of meat. The intestines are far too long to allow meat to pass through them effectively or speedily enough to promote an efficient evacuation process. This is detrimental to all that you will be trying to do with a living food approach. Whereas living foods feed the body and cleanse the system, meat can remain in the colon for a considerable length of time. It can go putrid. Meat and dairy products are dense and heavy (unlike plant based foods). They harbour high concentrations of saturated fats and proteins that are not health giving. They inhibit the evacuation process and they are considered by many to promote disease.

By the time meat and dairy produce has been turned into the processed end product e.g.

sausages, burgers, ice cream etc, they're highly likely to be packed full of additives/chemicals. These are alien to the natural process of the human body as it metabolises food. It is my understanding that vegans and vegetarians suffer much lower rates of cancer and heart disease. Nonetheless, we all have different metabolisms and it is important that you ensure you work with your particular needs. Moderation is always the best option if you feel unable to let go completely.

If and when you do let meat and dairy products go from your diet you are likely to notice the benefits very quickly. You will probably feel less inclined to want to return to eating these food types in any quantity when letting them go makes you feel so good.

If all this isn't enough to make you think twice before you choose to eat significant amounts of meat, the factory farming industry should certainly go a long way to helping you decide. The evidence tells us that animals are frequently dosed with antibiotics and growth hormones during factory farming production, kept in the most appalling conditions, and subjected to the most harrowing stress. The intensive farming of fish happens in the same way on densely populated fish farms. Do you really want to put all that into your body? Do you really want to carry this negative energy within you?

Even if you do not buy into letting go of meat and dairy products for the sake of animal welfare in the early stages of going raw, it's worth thinking very carefully about what you want to put into your body and the stress you are putting it under.

Once you are accustomed to eating living food you are likely to find the thought of eating dead flesh and heavy dairy produce less than pleasant. This is because your consciousness is raised and you start to 'feel' more in tune with the planet as you are eating the natural bounty the earth brings you. In all probability the very idea of eating dense, fatty produce will no longer appeal to you - especially when you notice the differences in your wellbeing and energy levels when you have let these food types go.

Why not try it and experience the difference for yourself? Why not consider replacing these proteins with pulses and seeds?

Re-educating your taste buds

As you eat more vibrant living foods you're likely to find your tastes change fairly quickly. Before long you begin to value the texture and taste of your food more. You enjoy the flavours more because you start to know the sensation of crisp, clean, unadulterated foods. Even if there are foods you're hanging onto (if you've decided to let most cooked and processed food go) don't worry about it. If you feel you want to eat some cooked or processed food when you've gone largely raw, this should not be seen as a problem. Check in with yourself and consider.

If you make the choice to eat a particular food you have let go from your diet - give yourself permission. Never beat yourself up for eating a food you have let go of but occasionally choose to eat - but always be sure to make your choices in a 'conscious' manner and accept them in harmony.

Hunger and reframing

Hunger, what hunger? There is no need for you to experience hunger when you eat living foods. Get hunger out of your life now. How? Simple. You can manage hunger by forgetting about it. You are not on a 'dieting' regime with living food. Living food should be enjoyable and fulfilling. It isn't about denial. It is about abundance, generosity, tuning in with the bounty of the earth and living life to the full.

If your body has been fed a diet lacking the nutrients it needs, hunger will be a common sensation to you. This is because the brain is constantly calling for nourishment for the body. As you nourish the body properly and it cleanses itself of toxins, it will stop continually crying out in hunger for the nourishment it has been lacking.

During the transition period you may find you experience what you believe to be hunger sensations. This can be for a number of reasons. Your body is used to sending messages to your brain asking for food because it's had to do this for a long time when you've fed it dead, lifeless matter - leaving it undernourished (hungry) for the food it really needs. If this happens, eat more. But eat more living foods!

Don't mistake these hunger calls as calls for the high sugar and fat food types you've ceased to eat, or now eat less of. You may want to enjoy more vegetable based juices as this gives you a higher concentration of enzymes and oxygen to feed your body with what it wants as it makes the transition to being well nourished. Or maybe you crave sugar. Eat fruit or make a lovely colourful fruit salad to satisfy your urge until your body has 'reframed'. You may be surprised at how little time it takes your body to reframe once you are feeding it what it really craves.

Further to this I fully agree with the theory Dr Batmanghelidj & Philip Day advance in their 2008 book - that many a hunger sensation is no more than the body calling for water due to a dehydrated state. As they illustrate, water is contained in food so the body sends hunger signals when it seeks rehydration.

If you rehydrate your body adequately you are likely to find you don't experience hunger pangs. If you think you feel hungry drink a glass of water and wait thirty minutes (as they suggest). This will enable you to work out whether you are hungry or just in need of hydration.

Because the brain is used to sending you hunger

pang signals a habit has developed. Habits can take a long time to break (approximately one to two months in my experience, depending on how entrenched they are). But it can be done. As you break the habit and allow your brain to 'reframe' be patient and be gentle on yourself.

Never go hungry! Smoothies, juices, fruit or a fruit salad, sliced vegetables with a little raw hummus dip, a glass of water - they all work as between meal helps if you need them. Or why not add a little carbohydrate using oat or rice cakes? If you truly have the intention to focus on your wellbeing with raw food and you feel the need to snack, you'll soon find it easier (and more pleasant) to feed yourself nourishing snacks than to reach for the sugary snacks.

Why not develop a new habit and take control of your eating now?

What helps if you feel the need for cooked food but want to go raw?

Some people find it much easier to eat raw food in warm weather. You may also feel the need for cooked food when you first start to increase your raw food and let go of your cooked food. Well, there isn't any need to feel hungry in cold weather when you are making the transition to a majority raw food intake. Nor is there any need to eliminate cooked food altogether on a mainly raw food intake. In cold weather you can spice your food up with plenty of the warming spices (add to lightly stir fried vegetables if you really feel the need for cooked food), or add plenty of ginger or other warming spices to your juices and smoothies.

Don't beat yourself up about it if you feel you need hot food. That's fine. Make yourself a hot soup (chop vegetables, add vegetable bouillon, 'cook' as little as possible leaving vegetables still firm, cool, blend - easy). If you do this, prepare your raw food and eat as normal onto an empty stomach, then use your soup as a winter warmer.

Don't forget you should be drinking plenty of fruit or herbal teas too (piping hot in winter). I sometimes drink a good proportion of my 2~3 litres water a day hot with lemon or lemon and fresh ginger in it.

Ancient societies believed that keeping the body warm came from within. They found that certain foods could raise the body's temperature. Long, long before processed foods arrived in our lives they used these foods to generate body heat naturally. Here are some of the foods they used:

- *Legumes*
- *Carrots*
- *Squash*
- *Parsnips*
- *Beetroot*
- *Walnuts, pine nuts*
- *Coconut*
- *Dates*
- *Red peppers and chillis*
  (list from Elaine Bruce's website)

Planning, managing and being in control of your food

I always think planning is an important stage of any change you make in your life. At some level, if you're making change, you have to plan how you'll do it. If you plan your shopping and the preparation and eating of your food it puts you in control and raises your conscious awareness around food.

Think about where and when you buy your food. Build a plan that fits in with your life. This will help to ensure your food is always fresh and that you have as much variety as you want.

Having organised yourself to make sure you always have plenty of fresh raw food on hand make sure you show yourself enough respect to allocate appropriate time for preparing and eating it. This may include setting time aside for experimental preparation and trying out new recipes.

CHAPTER EIGHT
LIVING FOODS AND SUSTAINABLE WEIGHT

It's not about being on a diet!

I can't stress enough that living foods for successful weight loss is not about being on a diet' in the familiar way we generally understand this concept.

It is about choosing to make changes in your life that will allow you to move forward into a different approach to weight loss and a different kind of lifestyle. It's about you taking control of what you eat and experiencing the wonderful freedoms and sense of empowerment that come with being in charge of your eating and the choices you make. It brings you amazing energy, confidence and wellbeing and this leads to massive knock on lifestyle changes.

If you aim to lose weight with living foods one of the best things you can do is forget about the weight loss issue altogether! Focus instead on how you feel inside (you may also want to re-read Chapter 4 on conscious eating at this point). As you start moving into a raw food eating pattern you will start to feel your positive energy growing. Focus on this.

Your weight is about your holistic self - mind, body, spirit and emotions. You are unlikely to ever fully address your weight issues in an effective and holistic way that allows you to let concerns about your weight go completely from your life until you accept this.

How much living food should you eat?

A good option when changing to living foods is to begin by replacing no more than 50% of the cooked and processed food you eat with vibrant, fresh, living foods. For example, you might have fresh fruit for breakfast instead of your usual breakfast (if you feel peckish to begin with mid morning just snack on more fresh fruit). Then you could introduce green salad with plenty of raw, fresh vegetables for lunch and still eat your usual evening meal.

You'll soon notice a difference if you take this approach. If you are overweight you will allow your body weight to decrease in a natural way and your energy will increase. This will spur you on to gradually replace more cooked and processed foods with living foods.

Increase your living food intake and decrease your intake of cooked and processed foods at the rate you are comfortable with. You are making a lifestyle change so take your time if you need to.

Once you reach a living food intake of 70% plus you will be feeling a vast difference in your energy levels. If your aim is weight loss you should find you are seeing excess weight start to drop off easily now. Some people never go above this percentage of living food as this is where they choose to find their balance, making up the remainder of their food intake with healthy option carbohydrates and proteins. Others are so rejuvenated they eat far higher percentages of raw food and prefer a low protein and carbohydrate intake.

Do what works for you. The most important thing is always that you feel the very best you can feel at any given time. Only you can judge how you feel and only you can choose how much raw food you need to eat.

Never go hungry again

With raw, water based food types (vegetables and fruits) eat as much as you feel you need. Don't stint! Never go hungry! If you allow yourself to feel hungry this will bring negative experience into your life and you are less likely to make a lifestyle change and more likely to feel you have to deny yourself food. This is a diet based attitude that's easy to relapse into. Let it go!

You may find, as you go raw, that you eat quite significant amounts of living food and the portion sizes are large in comparison to the portions 'allowed' on any of the 'diet' regimes you have subjected yourself to. Don't forget that living food is a lifestyle choice. Be gentle on yourself. If the portions of living green foods you feel you want to eat seem very large don't be concerned. Your body needs them.

My view is that you need to find out what works for you in terms of how much raw food you replace cooked and processed food with. Trust that you will find the place you need to be by listening to your body, taking control of your wellbeing and being honest with yourself. So, eat raw as you 'feel' you need and, above all, enjoy!

Living food should be truly enjoyed as a joyous part of your life. Taking a living food approach to weight loss or/and wellbeing is not about becoming an ascetic. It isn't about going without food or about feeling hungry. It is about you enjoying a life filled with vibrant energy at a weight you are truly happy with in a body you love. And it's about being the best you can be - that's what makes life fabulous. It's about you making the choices that ensure you are living the lifestyle that suits you.

How much weight can you expect to lose?

I include this section only because, in the beginning, you may still have a 'diet' mentality. In time, raw food eating patterns will help you let this go.

In the majority of cases weight loss is quite significant when you make the change to living foods (unless there is a medical reason preventing it). One of the common complaints I hear from people who are not overweight and make the transition to raw food for reasons of health and wellbeing is that they lose weight very quickly and too easily! They have trouble keeping weight on!

It's not uncommon for people to lose considerably more than three pounds a week as they go raw, but this does depend on many other factors and can only be considered on an individual basis. The more overweight you are, the more weight you are likely to lose when you start removing dead food and replacing it with nourishing living food.

Even if you only have a little weight to lose and you replace just 50% of your normal cooked and processed diet with the food types suggested for optimum weight loss (see next section 'Using Living Food for Optimum Weight Loss'), you can still expect to lose up to four pounds a week on average (over a month) and enjoy a great energy boost into the bargain. It's a win~win situation if you have a weight loss aim.

You are in control. With living food you will find you lose weight naturally and you will focus less on the body and more on how you feel and your holistic wellbeing.

Once you are in control of this you will naturally adjust your living food intake by using a variety of food combinations and ensuring you eat the amount of protein and carbohydrate foods you need to sustain holistic balance. This means you will 'manage' your weight without having to consider your physical body any more than being part of your overall health and wellbeing.

Using living foods for optimum weight loss

As always, when the aim is to lose weight the

qualified opinion of your chosen medical/health professional should always be sought. This is important because everyone is an individual with specific issues to manage and any changes to the diet can affect the holistic being.

In the beginning, if you are using living food to achieve optimum weight loss there are some key things to consider as you plan. The most important of these is the 'types' of living food you eat when you want to ensure maximum weight loss in a safe, healthy and effective manner.

When losing weight is a clear aim, water based foods (those listed in the vegetables, fruits, berries, herbs and spices categories in Appendix 1 should, temporarily, make up a significant proportion of your entire raw food intake.

Try to eat more vegetables than anything else. Your body will find it easy to metabolise vegetables. If you juice them, all the better. Juicing condenses the enzyme enriched goodness you give your body. In time, as you start to give your body the nutrients it needs, food cravings for toxic, cooked and processed foods will diminish. All of this assists optimum weight loss.

Herbs and spices may also be eaten freely. These are particularly useful in the early stages of transition to a raw food lifestyle when you may feel the need for something cooked. Whilst still adjusting to raw food you can lightly stir fry your vegetables in a small amount of oil and add herbs/spices for a variety of tastes. At first you may feel you want to actually bring your vegetables to the 'cooked' state. If this happens it's okay to go with it. Praise yourself for increasing your vegetable intake. You will be going in the right direction.

As time goes on and your tastes and liking for different textures adjust, you are likely to discover that you find yourself wanting your food to be more crisp and firm. As your palate changes, your body will detoxify. You'll begin to enjoy the texture and taste of your food more. In all probability you will soon reach a point where you realise you are cooking your stir fry so minimally it's not worth cooking it at all!

Because fresh fruits and berries contain a higher proportion of natural sugars than vegetables these should be your second living food priority in terms of intake. This means you can still eat them liberally with the exception of avocado, which is very nutritious but also high in fat. Although it is excellent nourishment it isn't the best thing to eat in quantity for weight loss!

Nevertheless, there is no need to exclude avocado completely because of the rich fat content.

Never cut out all fat from your diet. The body needs fats, but try to use pure olive, sesame, hemp or flax oil - not the heavy oils and fats. And certainly steer clear of fats and oils sourced from animals.

If weight loss is your goal, don't take a liberal approach to dried fruits! Because they've been dried the sugar content has been condensed and the water content extracted. Try to leave these out of the diet for the most part (temporarily) when weight loss is the primary aim. Alternatively, reduce them to a minimal intake.

Grains, beans, nuts and dried seeds are important. These should also be eaten in moderation. Foods listed in the 'other' section of the chart in Appendix 1 should be eaten in moderation whilst weight loss is a main aim. As you become more familiar with eating living food and listening to your body you will know how much or little you need.

Eating more grains and beans will slow weight loss down, eating more water based foods will speed weight loss up. Only you know how your body feels and the balance it needs for wellbeing.

Speedy weight loss is not always the most effective way to reach your weight loss goal. Seeing results quite quickly may be important as this can help keep you motivated on your weight loss journey, but sometimes the slow and steady approach is the most effective.

Using living food for weight loss and wellbeing is about a whole person journey. In many cases the steadier the pace the more permanent the results are likely to be. It can be helpful to see moving into a living food diet as a lifestyle change rather than a quick fix.

All of this means taking responsibility for your wellbeing as a long term commitment. As your body changes this allows you time to change and develop within yourself on other levels (emotional, spiritual and mental). Having said that, it's up to you how you choose to manage your journey into a slimmer, lighter, brighter future. You are the person who best knows how you want to shape your future.

In summary, you will maximise your weight loss if you:

◆ *eat as many water based vegetables (salad, cruciferous and other) as you like*
◆ *eat fresh fruits and berries liberally*
◆ *eat grains and beans in moderation and enjoy nuts and seeds more sparingly*
◆ *keep your intake of oils moderate (stick to flax, olive or hemp seed)*
◆ *try and eat fresh rather than dried fruits whilst weight loss is the main goal*

When you are happy with your body weight you can maintain it naturally on a living food diet with very little effort.

Your focus is your wellbeing, not your weight. As health and wellbeing come into focus the spiritual elements open up and the physical decline.

CHAPTER NINE
MAKING YOUR OWN CHOICES

THE SIMPLICITY OF IT ALL

You now know that there are the obvious basics to take on board when you decide to take the raw food approach. For example, your food should be fresh and is best when it's out of the ground and into your body with as little adulteration and as short a time scale as possible.

After that it's up to you to take responsibility for your choices. You have to sift the information you find and make our own decisions about what is categorised as living/raw food. Different commentators may have differing views on what they class as raw food. In general fresh fruit and vegetables, nuts, dried fruits and seeds, vegetable/seed based oils, and pulses are all counted as raw foods. But it really is for you to decide what your body needs. Will you dehydrate your food? Do you think raw chocolate should be included in your list? The main thing for all of us to do is to always make sure that what we eat makes us the best we can be every moment of every day of our lives. This means that for most of us the bulk of our intake needs to be 70-80% alkaline and as green as possible!

Some of us may choose (usually not to begin with) to dehydrate some of the food we eat and this can add extra variety to a living food diet in terms of taste, texture and shelf life. Whether you decide to eat a proportion of dehydrated food in your diet or not is up to you.

In fact, whatever you choose to do with your food is up to you. So remember that and make sure you stay in the driving seat. Making choices and taking control of your eating is incredibly empowering. For a balanced diet we all need other types of food as well as water based foods. Depending on our personal requirements, body types, blood types, and the choices we make, we will eat a variety of foods to varying degrees at different times.

Whatever choices you make try to always include a significant amount of water based raw fruit and vegetables daily for appropriate rehydration and optimum wellbeing and to assist with weight loss if this is an aim for you.

What you choose to include in your raw food diet is up to you. I urge you to experiment. You will find the balance that's right for you.

You are the person living inside your body and your body knows what's good for it! I'm not going to give you a prescription for what you should and shouldn't be eating on a raw/living food diet. This is something you will soon work out for yourself, according to your needs. If you listen to your body, it will tell you what it needs.

Listening to your holistic self and respecting your holistic needs

You can develop the habit! Trust in this. Connect with your body, mind, spirit and emotions and they will tell you all you need to know to be the best you can be.

Sounds simple doesn't it? Well, like anything else, it is...once you get the hang of it. I look at it like this. Food is the fuel we give our bodies. We need the best possible fuel if we're going to get the best we possibly can from our bodies. Our bodies are where our mind, emotions and soul live. The best possible fuel for one person may not be the best possible fuel for another! Your body will tell you - by the reaction it gives - what's good for you as a whole person... and what's not. It's up to you to listen.

If you're overweight, tired most of the time, skin dull, hair out of condition, poor complexion, mind not focused, you can be fairly sure that the fuel you're putting in isn't the best fuel for you. As you get older poor nutrition compounds these things. But it doesn't have to if you make the changes you know you need to make.

Each of us is a wondrous compilation of body, mind, spirit and emotions. Listening to your body, mind, spirit and emotions - I mean really listening, honestly with yourself, will tell you when any aspect of 'you' is out of balance. Listening will definitely tell you when the fuel is wrong and you are filling your body with the wrong amount of food. You only have to recall a few of those huge festive meals you've had at Christmas and how you felt after them. You've been there - you know what I'm talking about. So, you see, it's not so difficult to tune in and 'listen'.

CHAPTER TEN
HAVING THE CONFIDENCE TO CHANGE

The most effective way to increase your confidence is to be in control of all elements of your life in a positive way and be open to opportunity.

Here are some things you can do as you start changing your way of eating, taking control of the choices you make, and moving into the freedom of a raw food lifestyle:

Smile and hold your head up... you will be amazed at how your confidence can increase inwardly when you look confident on the outside. I'm told that smiling also produces a chemical reaction - one that makes us feel good

Take a few moments to breathe deeply at regular intervals throughout the day. This will help you centre yourself and slow you down as it fills your body with oxygen and clears your head

Learn to say no when you don't want to do something. In the early days of going raw this is a must as some people will almost definitely challenge your decision to introduce more raw food into your diet. Tell them if you do not want cooked food and gently explain that this is your decision to make, not theirs

Know that everything is as it should be at any

given moment and therefore you can accept it as it is and you are in control in that acceptance

Just some of the benefits of going more raw

It is widely reported that people changing to a high raw food lifestyle experience considerable holistic benefits. These reportedly range from a full recovery from illness and/or disease (mental, emotional and/or physical) as the body rebalances, to minor improvements in health and wellbeing.

Here are some of the benefits most commonly experienced:

- *Clearer thinking*
- *Improved memory and concentration*
- *More energy and natural weight loss*
- *Quality of sleep improves*
- *Rejuvenation and spiritual expansion*
- *Reversal of signs of ageing*
- *Stronger immune system*
- *Sparkling eyes! No more dark circles!*
- *Clearer, smoother skin*
- *Shiny, glossier hair*
- *Less/no coughs and colds*
- *Excess mucus in lungs and nose clears*
- *Less/no eczema, hay fever, asthma*

- *No more headaches or period pains*
- *No more constipation*
- *No more irritable bowel syndrome*
- *No more indigestion/heartburn*
- *Healing of disease*

And of course, the feeling that, at last, personal potential can be achieved. All of the above increase self-confidence and reaffirm the sense of self love.

Information overload!

There is a vast amount of information about raw food on the internet and elsewhere. As you investigate further please remember that discussion is always healthy. However, I urge you to consider any information and advice that comes your way (including the information in this short book) and accept or discard it as you choose. You are in control. Take responsibility for yourself and your lifestyle and base your choices on what you feel is best for you.

It's good to respect the views and ideas of others. It's also good to remember that the basic principles of a living food lifestyle are open to us all and need cost us very little financially. There is enough free information out there for us to link into and learn from. You don't need to spend lots of money to adjust to a liberating raw food lifestyle. You simply need to 'reframe' your world view at the pace you choose.

Being open to opportunity

To get the best out of the raw 'approach' to improved holistic wellbeing I recommend that you open your mind, body, spirit and emotions to change. You are reading this because you want to make a change in your life. Open up to the opportunities the transformation to living food brings your way. If you do this, I'm confident that you will discover the raw food lifestyle bringing you many more opportunities than you anticipate, on many more levels than you expect!

The opportunities for choices and change that offer the potential for personal growth are likely to come your way in remarkable abundance as you reframe your world. They will arise on many levels - mind, body, spirit and emotions. Doors open because living food cleanses holistically. It's up to you how many open doors you choose to walk through.

All change begins with thought. Live confidently in the knowledge that, when you are in charge of your world, when you are taking responsibility for your holistic 'self', you will live in the power of your own choices.

My own living food journey has been both transformational and inspirational.

You have the opportunity to transform your life with living food.

Remember...

The choices you make should always be yours! You, and only you, are responsible for your holistic wellbeing!

You are the creator of your world!

APPENDIX 1

FOOD LIST
WHAT COUNTS AS LIVING FOOD?

The foods listed in each category are by no means exhaustive. They give you an idea of some of the key foods you are likely to introduce or increase as you let go cooked/processed foods. Within their categories, they are not listed in any special order - mix and match! Enjoy!

VEGETABLES

Carrots, Cabbage, Spinach, Broccoli, Cucumber, Peppers, Fennel, Cauliflower, Green beans, Sweet corn, Silver beet, Chives, Lettuce, Onions, Mushrooms, Peas, Asparagus, Kale, Artichoke, Aubergine, Seaweed, Chard, Watercress, Celeriac, Endive, Courgette, Radish, Beetroot, Broad beans, Cress, Chicory, Celery, Salad leaves, Olives, Kumara

FRUITS

Apple, Orange, Pear, Banana, Lemon, Lime, Fig, Apricot, Grapefruit, Peach, Plum, Grapes, Mango, Quince, Pineapple, Cherry, Kiwi fruit, Papaya, Pawpaw, Cumquat, Tangerine, Mandarin, Cherimoya, Tomato, Nectarine, Rhubarb, Melon, Watermelon, Pomegranate, Avocado, Sun dried tomato

DRIED FRUIT

Durian, Raisins, Dates, Figs, Prunes, Apricots

GRAINS & BEANS

Wheat(grass), Wild rice, Millet, Wholegrain rice, Mung, Black eye, Buckwheat, Quinoa, Lentils, Chickpeas, Aduki

BERRIES

Strawberry, Raspberry, Redcurrant, Gooseberry, Loganberry, Blackcurrant, Mulberry, Blueberry, Blackberry, Cranberry, Goji

HERBS & SPICES

Ginger, Garlic, Cumin, Dill, Mint, Parsley, Rosemary, Thyme, Sage, Basil, Coriander, Cayenne pepper, Chilli, Sea salt, Oregano, Turmeric, Nutmeg, Cilantro, Paprika, Pepper

OTHER

Olive, almond, flax, walnut, agave, tahini, honey, hemp oils, tamar sauce, almond butter, agave, tahini

ABOUT THE AUTHOR

This brief outline of how I came to living food is a little of my own personal truth and learning that I share with you. In 2002 when I was backpacking in New Zealand I became ill. At that time I also met an organic farmer. She was to become the person who taught me the value of living food and how to use it for healing. I little realised then that she had set me on a life changing path.

Medics advised that I return to the UK for surgery - so I did. I went back to work whilst in the first stages of my raw food journey. Despite significant objections from those who loved me (and only knew the medical model for healing) I knew my body 'felt' well being nourished with living food, so I chose to trust my intuition and go with the raw option.

As I became well I also experienced a huge shift in my sense of increased overall wellbeing. It took me eighteen months to fully heal my body and I never had that operation!

However, other massive and unforeseen benefits also came into my life! My lifelong struggle with my weight vanished from my world! More than that - my whole world changed! I became a healthy person in many other ways on many other levels. I now lead a fabulous lifestyle free from weight concerns where I am in control of my world and my wellbeing.

My mission is to share the benefits of living food with others - because anyone who chooses to do so can have a future filled with increased wellbeing.

It's a great space to live in!